PRINCE WILLIAM

PRINCE WILLIAM

Valerie Garner

BENFORD BOOKS

PRINCETON, NEW JERSEY

PRINCE WILLIAM

Prince William is second in line to the throne and is destined to become King of England, Scotland, Wales, Northern Ireland and the Commonwealth, Head of the Church of England and the armed forces.

Tall, blond and athletic, the eldest son of the Prince of Wales and the late Diana, Princess of Wales has emerged from the emotional traumas of his early teenage years, which culminated in his mother's tragic death, with a self-reliant maturity unusual in one so young.

At sixteen he finds himself, to his huge embarrassment, becoming a pin-up superstar after a tumultuous welcome in Canada from crowds composed mainly of teenage girls. They greeted him with the screams of excitement normally reserved for film and rock stars and the frenzied scenes appeared in the media worldwide.

'I love him so much,' said one girl. 'Look at him. He's royalty. He's so hot, I've got posters of him all over my bedroom.' Last St Valentine's Day William received mailbags full of Valentine cards. One teenage magazine editor even thought up the idea of giving away 250,000 'I love Willy' stickers, explaining that he was 'classic boyfriend material'.

Despite this baptism of fire William is still inclined to be withdrawn and

WILLIAM IT'S ME
♥ YOU'VE BEEN
LOOKING FOR

What young man could resist an invitation like this? Teenage girls waiting for the Prince to arrive in Vancouver, March 1998.

diffident at times. He already has glamour because of who he is and it is becoming clear that his brand of casual good looks and easy charm is proving irresistible to young women.

He has his mother's cornflower blue eyes and friendly smile and more than a hint of Spencer red in his hair. He also has a low-pitched, well-modulated

voice and Diana's gift of making whoever he meets feel important to him, as mourners outside Kensington Palace found when, immersed with grief himself, he spoke to them as she would have done and somehow even managed to smile.

Michael Shea, one of the Queen's most trusted courtiers during his years at Buckingham Palace, used to say that starring roles in the Royal Family shifted little by little from one leading royal to another. In William's case it has been an abrupt but very natural transition from the now almost legendary Diana to the son who is hauntingly like her in looks and mannerisms.

His efforts at socializing in public, like the time he attended a party at a Hammersmith nightclub with a group of school friends, have not been successful. For once it was not just the media to blame. Teenage girls surrounded him asking for kisses and he spent most of the evening trying to get away from them. He had a miserable time, as did his friends, who felt bound to help him. The whole performance was, to the Prince's dismay, a gift for the tabloids.

Wiser heads in the Royal Family might well have said that the situation in a public nightspot was entirely predictable and it is unlikely that William will repeat the experience, at least until he is older. He prefers private parties with hosts he can trust not to talk to newspapers or magazines. There are plenty of those, some in more exotic venues than a London nightclub. Mr Mohammed al Fayed even organized one of the smartest discos in the South

of France to entertain William and his brother Harry privately when they were his guests in St Tropez. But that is another experience that is unlikely to be repeated.

Since his appearance triggered off such frenzied acclaim from his own generation William has also acquired a higher profile within the Royal Family which, headed by his grandmother, the Queen, has gathered protectively around him. Within this circle William, who towers above most of them at over six feet tall, is already very much his own man and growing rapidly into a strong and confident young adult.

Disciplined and more serious than smiling pictures reveal, he appears older than his school friends of the same age. But none of them have grown up as fast as the Prince in a year so full of personal grief and change. He is now consulted on all aspects of his life and is already, perhaps unconsciously, pioneering a new breed of royal with the style of his mother and the self-control of the Windsors.

Said by genealogists to be the most British prince for centuries, William's modern outlook seems tailored for the new century in which the pace will be faster and the mood more radical. With high-tech communications already in their lives William's age group are coming to adulthood earlier. The Establishment led by Prime Minister Tony Blair is more inclined to listen to the young and the Prince of Wales has heeded with interest and sensitivity the views of his elder son who found the scenes after his mother's death in August 1997 both intensely moving and thought-provoking.

William today is living in two worlds. There is school at Eton College, Windsor, where he is treated like any other pupil except that he has a private detective and goes to tea with the Queen on Sunday afternoons at 'the castle on the hill'. There are also holidays at Highgrove, his home in Gloucestershire, or any of the royal estates where he is a guest of his grandparents. His other world in which he still moves warily and reluctantly, is one of crowds and staring faces and the cameras that will forever mirror his public life. Like any young man would, he finds adulation embarrassing and his mother's legacy of aversion to unknown photographers still haunts him. Prince Charles, no stranger to these feelings, is gradually trying to coax him back to facing the cameras. 'But he does have a serious

problem with photographers,' acknowledged Jayne Fincher, whom William knows well and trusts since she was invited to photograph him with his parents and brother at an informal session at Highgrove. On that occasion Jayne had the foresight to arrive equipped with false red noses and funny hats, which Prince Charles obligingly wore and had his sons falling about with laughter. The result was a picture that became a royal favourite. But that was in private in the garden of his home. International publicity is something else but it is a prospect that a prince with privilege and future responsibility of the most awesome kind must become acclimatized to if the monarchy is to survive in a more demanding and republican world.

Despite his growing confidence and the strength he can find when he needs it, as he did at his mother's funeral, William is still very vulnerable. His cousin Freddy (Lord Frederick Windsor, son of Prince and Princess Michael of Kent) knew this when he acted as chief unofficial bodyguard one afternoon at the Guard's Polo Club, Windsor. Eton boys traditionally serve tea to members of the Royal Family at the club during Ascot Week. William

A loving trio. But however close they were to their mother the boys always knew they were loved by both their parents. 'If a family breaks up the problems created can still be resolved.' said the Princess. 'But only if the children have been brought up from the start with the feeling that they are wanted, loved and valued'.

arrived by the back entrance to the royal pavilion and tried to keep out of sight of the cameras. When he finally appeared outside, his school friends, orchestrated by Freddy, formed a circle round the Prince who kept his distinctive blond head well down and was indistinguishable from the others in their black and white Etonian uniform. It gave him some respite and 'time to scoff all the cakes' as one of them put it. Finally the Prince of Wales decided the time had come for William to face up to the cameras and marched his son out of the front entrance. William is tall and inclined to do the old trick so reminiscent of his mother in the early days, of hanging his head to disguise his height. Again, like Diana, he blushes easily. 'Put your head up Wills,' shouted the rat-pack. Reluctantly he did.

Cameras first followed Prince William's progress soon after his birth on 21 June 1982, when he left St Mary's Hospital, Paddington, in his mother's arms to go home to Kensington Palace. He was born in the Lindo Wing, the first baby so close to the throne to be born in hospital. They put a band around his wrist with 'Baby Wales' written on it.

Mr George Pinker (later Sir), the Surgeon Gynaecologist to the Queen, and the four nurses who looked after William were guests of honour at his christening in the Music Room of Buckingham Palace. William distinguished himself by howling after the ceremony as photographs were being taken and his mother soothed him by letting him suck her little finger. 'He certainly has a good set of lungs,' observed his great-grandmother, the Queen Mother, whose eighty-second birthday it was.

William's next photocall was in New Zealand on a visit with his parents the following March – an unprecedented trip for a nine-month-old royal baby. He crawled for the cameras, unconcerned and amiable. There was no sign of the Windsor/Spencer temper he is said to have inherited when exasperated. 'He gets noisier and angrier by the day,' his father had remarked when he was a few weeks old.

Earlier in the visit the Prince and Princess toured Australia where they nicknamed William 'Billy the Kid'. As his parents began their visit he was taken with his nanny, Barbara Barnes, to Woomargama, a four-thousand-acre sheep station in New South Wales far away from the crowds and the

The Prince, who adores speed, enjoys the Log Flume on a visit to Thorpe Park with his mother and brother.

photographers. The Prince and Princess returned every few days to see him at this safe haven. Since then, throughout William's young life, efforts have been made to try and make his world less claustrophobic. 'Like living in a goldfish bowl,' the Duke of Edinburgh once described life as a royal.

His early years at school, first at Mrs Mynor's nursery school, next at Wetherby in London's Notting Hill and then boarding at Ludgrove in Berkshire, formed a shield against the outside world and 'Wills', as his family call him, lived the normal life of any eight-to thirteen-year-old boy away at boarding school. For his first half-term holiday he was taken to Alton Towers

theme park in Staffordshire with his brother Harry, two years his junior, and a party which included the children of his mother's butler, chauffeur and maid. This royal party, headed by Diana, queued with everyone else, rejecting any special treatment and ended up soaked after trying all the rides including the Log Flume and Rapids Ride. William and Harry eventually braved real rapids later on a holiday in Colorado when they went white water rafting with their mother on one of her 'fun hols'.

Only his parent's marriage worried William. It was becoming increasingly stormy and he hated to see his mother in tears. Once she reportedly shut

12

herself in the bathroom and William, anxious to comfort her, shoved tissues under the bathroom door when he heard her crying.

The media mainly responded to a plea for privacy for both boys away at school, but in June 1991 there was one story they could not ignore. The future King William V was rushed to hospital after an unfortunate fellow pupil accidentally hit him on the head with a golf club. 'My heart went cold,' his father said when he heard the news. But at the Royal Berkshire Hospital it turned out not to be so serious. There was a small indentation on William's head and he

was taken by ambulance to the Great Ormond Street Hospital for Sick Children in London for what was described as 'a routine operation'.

The following year William's progress at Ludgrove was not as good as it should have been. It was possible that his parent's turbulent marriage was having an effect on his work. It came as no surprise to those close to the couple when later in the year, in December 1992, their separation was announced by John Major, the Prime Minister of the day, in the House of Commons. Earlier the Princess had contacted Gerald Barber, the headmaster of Ludgrove

Showing a love of horses that delights his grandmother, the Queen, and his great-grandmother, the Queen Mother, William, aged eleven, at a Christmas show-jumping performance at Olympia.

Prince William on his first day at Eton.

to warn him she would be coming to see William and Harry, who by then had joined his brother at the school. With the help of Jane Barber, the headmaster's wife, she broke the news to her sons. Both youngsters were said to have reacted differently. William, the sensitive one, older and more aware of the implications of the news than his younger brother was in tears; Harry just bewildered. Since then the boys, who used to fight a lot, have been closer than most siblings, with William, the kind-hearted elder brother being especially protective of Harry. Shuttling between two homes, however carefully the visits were organized, was always an emotional strain. But it was one they shared, which made it easier for both of them.

Diana herself revealed something of William's attitude to the subsequent divorce when she said: 'Well, he's a child that's a deep thinker and we won't know for a few years how it has gone in. But I put it in gently without any resentment or anger.'

After the separation and divorce the Princes' holidays became, however unintended, almost a competition between their parents. Prince Charles took them on skiing holidays to Klosters, on luxury cruises to the Mediterranean and on safari to Africa. Their mother took them to the West Indies, the Rocky Mountains, America and that ill-fated holiday to the South of France where she fell in love with Dodi Fayed.

When William went to Eton there was another hated photocall as he signed the roll-book and the world saw that he appeared to be left-handed. Afterwards the media, obedient to the 'no intrusion' edict agreed with editors, withdrew and a new phase in William's life began.

Eton seems to be the perfect choice for the young Prince. Founded in 1440 by King Henry VI, it has a distinctive uniform of black tail coats, waistcoats, pin-striped trousers, wing collars and bow ties, which goes back to the day the school went into mourning clothes for William's ancestor, King George III, in 1820. Like all his school friends, however, he cannot wait to cast these clothes aside whenever possible. He relaxes in trendy lounging gear, described by one of his contemporaries as 'something baggy, soft and slouchy', an anathema to Prince Charles who likes to see his boys in flannels and sports jackets or blazers.

William is beginning his fourth year at Eton, the start of his two senior years. He has a study-bedroom in Manor House, a four-storey ivy-clad building not far from the public road. The back-up team running Manor House has helped him greatly in the past year. Headed by his housemaster Andrew Gailey, forty-three, and his wife Shauna, the team comprises Christopher

Stuart-Clark, his tutor, and Elizabeth Heathcote, the matron. A gentle comforter of homesick boys, 'the Dame', as she is known, is the daughter of an old Etonian. She tries to give her charges a touch of home in an all-male environment and her invitations to watch television in her flat or 'come to coffee' after Sunday lunch are very popular.

William has good friends in his House, including three boys who were with him at Ludgrove: Andrew Charlton, John Richards and Harry Walsh, who was Captain of Ludgrove in William's day. Their scholastic progress is always watched but in William's case it is being especially carefully monitored as it is likely to be an indication of how he is settling down and coping with the loss of his mother. He should be studying for his 'A' level subjects if all is well with his remaining GCSE results. His tutor, a young English teacher, looks after his day-by-day 'academic performance and intellectual development' and helps with any problems he may have.

Most important, for the Royal Family, Eton has tradition and discretion and is well suited to royalty. School regulations state: 'No boy may give information or contribute photographs,

articles, letters etc. to any journalist or publication.' This avoids the situation Prince Charles was confronted with at Gordonstoun, when his exercise book was stolen from a classroom and found its way to Fleet Street. It contained essays that were hawked around the world and published under the headline: 'The Confessions of Prince Charles'. They revealed nothing scandalous, however, just the musings of an enlightened boy of sixteen. It is of interest that, in one essay, he argued for a free press, which was essential in a democracy 'to protect people from the government in many ways, to let them know what is going on – perhaps behind their backs'.

Traditional it may be and centuries old, but Eton is about to launch itself into the high-tech age with its own public Internet site. 'But there will be no gossip about Prince William on it,' a spokesman said severely.

Sport, at which the Prince excels, is considered very important. Hence the saying that the Battle of Waterloo was 'won on the playing fields of Eton'. Because of this famous sporting tradition time off from studies is always strenuous. As well as the field sports he participates in on the royal estates and

FACING PAGE
Leaving a restaurant in July 1997, William spots a photographer and hangs his head to his mother's amusement. It was the way she used to react when she first hit the headlines as a prospective bride for Prince Charles.

17

at the country homes of friends, 'Wills' is an all-rounder. He enjoys playing football, skiing, cycling and nowadays is learning to become a 'wet bob', the Eton slang for an oarsman. But swimming is rapidly becoming his favourite sport and, like his mother, he is a natural in the water. He is recently reported to have beaten Eton's school record for the fifty-metre crawl with a time approaching a championship record. He may well decide to concentrate on his swimming because he is close to becoming one of Britain's top young swimmers. Like his aunt, the Princess Royal, who rode for Britain and her son, Peter Phillips, who played rugby in a Scottish junior team, William may one day be good enough to represent his country at swimming.

Especially delighted at his swimming prowess are the Queen and the Duke of Edinburgh, who have recently invested in a swimming pool for Sandringham as well as other royal homes.

William loves speed and motor-racing is a passion he shares with his brother. He cannot yet legally drive, except on private roads, so go-karting fills the gap. He once clocked up the fastest speed of the day at his local track in London, where racing drivers some-times relax. The Prince drove one of the 163cc go-karts to a lap record of 19.6 seconds. 'He has a very good attitude to racing,' said a track official. 'He is relaxed, not a white knuckle driver. In fact he is pretty cool.' At the track with William that day were 'speed kings' Damon Hill, Barry Sheene and David Coulthard. But maybe they were just having an 'off day'.

All royal youngsters learn to drive early on the private roads of the royal estates. Before he takes his driving test the Prince will have final lessons with a police driver or one of the royal chauffeurs. He will also learn anti-terrorist tactics, as all the royals do.

Always available to give advice, although not necessarily about go-karting, is John Major, legal guardian to both boys and becoming, increasingly, William's guru. Kindly and wise, the former Premier helped the Prince and Princess of Wales through their divorce and Diana was particularly fond of him, as William knows. He is, whenever possible, a shoulder for the Prince to lean on, someone outside the family whom he can consult.

Also at the other end of a telephone or fax is William's uncle, Earl Spencer, who vowed at his sister's funeral to

ensure that William's and Harry's souls were 'not simply immersed by duty and tradition but can sing openly as [you] planned'. There are also close links with Diana's two sisters, Lady Sarah McCorquodale and Lady Jane Fellowes, wife of the Queen's Private Secretary. Both William and Harry enjoy visiting their homes and spending time with their six cousins. The sisters, who were both very close to Diana, try to help balance her sons' royal training with the kind of humanitarian background the Princess wanted for her boys. 'I want them to have an understanding of people's emotions, of people's insecurities, of people's distress, of their hopes and dreams,' she once said.

It was as well that William had been prepared by his mother on issues of life and death. A friend who saw him visiting a dying man with the Princess noticed how mature and aware he was about terminal illness. As Diana mentioned in her *Panorama* interview: 'I take William and Harry round homelessness projects, I've taken them to people dying of AIDS albeit I told them it was cancer. I've taken the children to all sorts of areas where I'm not sure anyone of that age in this family has been before. And they have a

knowledge – they may never use it, but the seed is there and I hope it will grow because knowledge is power.'

After the Princess's death, William and his brother went sorrowfully back to Kensington Palace to choose mementoes from her collection of cuddly toys, most of them from her childhood, which she had still loved and kept on a sofa in her bedroom. There were pottery animals, too, and the small china boxes she used to collect. They took some of these treasures back to their new London home in St James's Palace where their bedrooms have been faithfully copied from those at Kensington Palace, even down to lifting the carpets.

Most weekends and part of the school holidays are spent at Highgrove, the home William loves. He and Harry have known the peaceful old Georgian house all their lives and, like their father, look on it almost as a sanctuary where they can be completely private. Now, in the former day and night nurseries where Bugs Bunny murals used to delight them, there are posters of pop and sports stars and all the paraphernalia of teenage occupants. Highgrove also houses their racing bikes, roller blades and the portable goal posts they

FACING PAGE

William, smartly turned out for the Queen Mother's birthday lunch for the family on 4 August 1995. If the weather is fine she likes to hold it under the trees in the Clarence House garden.

Prince William with the Queen Mother's faithful steward, William Tallon, outside Clarence House on her birthday.

is still at Gordonstoun. When they are all at home they see each other often and Zara joined the Prince of Wales's party at Klosters last year. Peter and William get together at Balmoral or Sandringham where they both love the shooting. The Duke of Edinburgh is delighted with these two grandsons who are young men after his own heart. Peter has been a staunch friend to William, who sticks close to him whenever the Royal Family appears together in public, and he was there to help ease the first few heart-breaking days at the Queen's Highland home as William and Harry tried to come to terms with their mother's death. Although untitled, the Princess Royal's son understands only too well the problems of being a member of the Royal Family.

rarely travel without, with which to practise their football. There is also a swimming pool and tennis courts.

Highgrove is only eight miles from Gatcombe Park, home of the Princess Royal and her family. William is especially fond of his cousins, Peter and Zara Phillips, who are more like elder brother and sister to the Wales boys. Peter, nearly twenty-one, is a student at Exeter University and Zara, seventeen,

There is none of the formality of their grandmother's residences about Highgrove. The boys can be as boisterous as any others of the same age and this is rarely curbed. Often the Prince of Wales joins in with their games and, in the privacy of their home, there is plenty of affection and understanding.

William has learnt the ways of the countryside from his father. Sometimes, when out walking or riding, Prince

PREVIOUS PAGE

Zara Phillips teases William, who is carrying a bouquet of flowers which had been presented by a well-wisher, during a visit to the Naval College at Greenwich, November 1997.

FACING PAGE

William and Harry laughing at the antics of photographers as they scramble over the rocks on the riverside at Balmoral in August 1997, only a few days before they heard the news of their mother's death.

Charles might talk to him about his future. He has been aware for some time that he will, unless there is radical constitutional change, one day be King. As his father once said: 'This just dawns on you slowly. You get the idea you have a certain duty and responsibility.' His brother put it more bluntly. When William said, some years ago, that he wanted to be a policeman when he grew up so that he could protect his mother, Harry said: 'You can't. You've got to be King.'

Now that William is older, Prince Charles is steering him into an appreciation of not just pop music but classical music, too. He also has a small part in the school Shakespeare play and now goes to Stratford-upon-Avon, the bard's birthplace with his father and Harry to watch performances by the Royal Shakespeare Company. Afterwards they go backstage to meet the players and sometimes have a snack in the theatre restaurant. To balance the classical, Prince Charles takes them to see the Spice Girls and Australian Barry Humphries, alias eye-flashing Dame Edna, whom they all enjoy.

It is clear at this pivotal point in their lives that William and Harry are growing increasingly close to their father. When he cannot be with them he calls on the help of thirty-one-year-old Alexandra Legge-Bourke, whose mother is lady-in-waiting to the Princess Royal. The Royal Family call her 'Tiggy' because she once worked at Mrs Tiggywinkle's nursery school in London. The boys love her easy-going, warm nature and the comfortable, relaxed ambience she always creates. William chose her instead of his parents to attend a Fourth of June celebration at Eton, reckoning she would cause 'much less fuss'. She and her two charges are a familiar sight in Tetbury, the town nearest Highgrove, where they go to buy ice-cream and the science-fiction books and magazines they love.

'Tiggy' goes on winter sports holidays with them, too. Also in the party in recent years, to William's delight, has been family friend and glamorous model Tara Palmer-Tomkinson who, with her elder sister Santa, has also accompanied Prince Charles and his sons on a summer cruise through the Greek islands.

William once had pin-up pictures of supermodel Cindy Crawford in his room. Now it is just as likely to be Tara or whichever girl is his fancy of the moment.

Towards the end of 1996, William heard his mother complaining that her wardrobes were overflowing and suggested she auction some of her dresses for charity. As a result, three-and-a-half million pounds were raised in New York for cancer and AIDS charities. 'It was all down to William,' said the Princess. 'It was his idea.'

After experiencing the 'Willsmania' of teenage girls in Vancouver he can expect to attract increasing world attention as he approaches the milestone of his eighteenth birthday. Then, the Queen may appoint him a Counsellor of State as she did his father at the same age. This means that, as one of those closest to the Succession, he will be authorized to act for the Queen if she is ill or out of the country. But, more likely, he may take a year's sabbatical in one of the commonwealth countries before going on to university. It is likely to be Trinity College, Cambridge, where his father was a student. But there is always the possibility he may go to Oxford like his great-great-great-grandfather King Edward VII. Dr Eric Anderson, Prince Charles's old friend and tutor at Gordonstoun (later Tony Blair's housemaster at Fettes, and eventually headmaster of Eton) is now Rector of Lincoln College, Oxford. After university there will be, if tradition is observed, a spell in one or all of the armed forces.

Growing up is difficult enough for an ordinary teenager, but coming to adulthood in the full glare of the world spotlight must be a difficult and demanding experience. We have yet to see whether William can detach himself from the restricting shadows of Palace protocol that so stifled Prince Charles as a young man. His mother told *New Yorker* Editor, Tina Brown, shortly before she died: 'All my hopes are on William now. I try to dim it into him about the media – the dangers and how he must understand and handle it. It's too late for the rest of the family. But William, I think he has it.'

No one who saw them will easily forget the sight of those two young boys walking with their father, grandfather and uncle behind their mother's coffin. In Prince Charles's words they were 'unbelievably brave', all through that long late summer's day. Some steel may well have been forged then in Diana's gentle elder son, which will help him as the Royal Family steers a course through the uncharted territory of the new millennium.

ABOVE *Prince Charles described his baby son as having 'a wisp of fair hair, sort of blondish, and blue eyes'.*

LEFT *Outside Paddington Hospital a delighted Prince and Princess of Wales admire their new-born son and heir as they prepare to take him home to Kensington Palace.*

Toddler Prince William, cosily wrapped up, goes walkabout.

The first of many appearances on the balcony at Buckingham Palace. William in his father's arms with his great-grandmother, the Queen Mother, and great-aunt, Princess Margaret.

Examining the mysteries of some photographic equipment. But as he grew older press cameras grew less interesting.

William aged two, looking remarkably like his father at the same age.

Prince William swiftly got bored at his brother's christening and took action of his own. 'Every time he did something naughty they roared with laughter,' said one of Lord Snowdon's assistants. 'He was being a thorough pest.'

LEFT *Being photographed was still interesting in those faraway toddler days. Now it's becoming all too familiar.*

ABOVE *First day at school in September 1985 when he was three. He chose his outfit of red shorts and checked shirt himself. 'It is best to let him,' said his mother, 'then he might smile for the cameras.'*

ABOVE *Prince William with his mother on the steps of the King and Queen of Spain's palace on Majorca where the Wales family had several happy holidays before their separation. Behind them is the Queen of Spain.*

RIGHT *William and Harry look pensive and rather bored on the steps of the King and Queen of Spain's palace. Clearly they'd rather be on the beach.*

LEFT *Reluctantly to school. Holidays are over and William with his brand-new satchel and grey and red uniform starts his first day at Wetherby.*

RIGHT *William and Harry in their Wetherby school uniforms. Their mother said her life was empty when they both went to school.*

*William, a future Prince of Wales,
wears a daffodil in his lapel as he visits
the Principality with his parents on
St David's Day.*

*Aged nine, the boy who will one day be
Head of the Church of England meets one
of its dignitaries, Easter 1991.*

'Now this is what I call fun,' Prince William seems to be saying as he tries on a fireman's helmet and has a ride on a fire engine.

William adores go-karting and has clocked up a record time at his local track. 'He is relaxed, not a white knuckle driver,' said an official.

ABOVE *Diana with William, aged twelve, and Harry, ten. She liked nothing better than to curl up with them in the evening in her sitting room and watch television.*

LEFT *Prince William helps his grandmother, the Queen, with the bouquets of flowers presented to her outside Sandringham Church on Christmas morning.*

ABOVE *William is beginning to love the fantastic scenery of the Swiss Alps as much as his father. Here they sit in a chair-lift on holiday at Klosters.*

RIGHT *William and Harry with their cousins Beatrice and Eugenie, daughters of the Duke and Duchess of York. The four were on a skiing holiday at Klosters with their mothers.*

LEFT *William and Harry aboard* Britannia *for VJ day anniversary celebrations, July 1995.*

ABOVE *It has been a long day and both Princes study their watches, sitting on the VIP stand in the Mall for the VJ day celebrations.*

ABOVE *This is how the Prince of Wales likes to see his son: in smart sports jacket and flannels.*

RIGHT *Prince William with his parents meets disabled ex-service men and women outside Buckingham Palace on VJ day.*

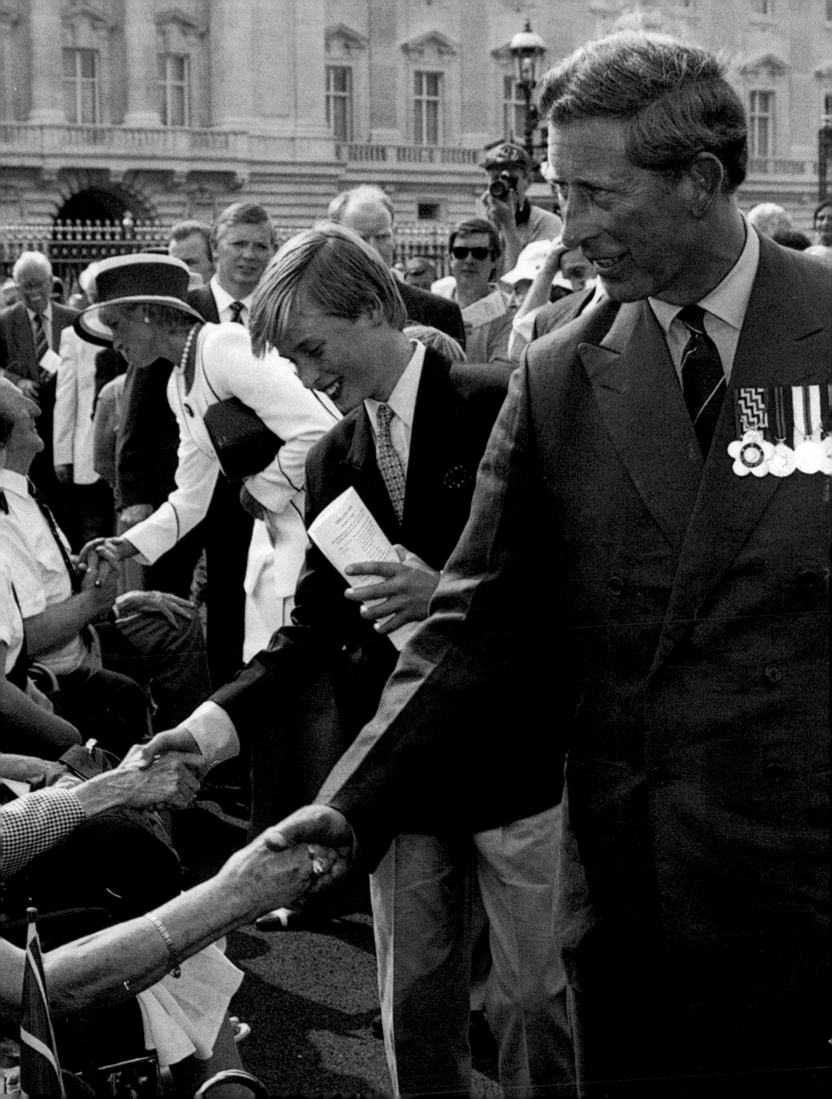

Fun time. William and a friend at a fair in the town of Tetbury.

LEFT *Behind that smile so like his mother's, William is, in Diana's words, 'a deep thinker'.*

Eton College. Founded in 1440 by King Henry VI, it has educated royalty, Prime Ministers and statesmen in its ancient buildings. Now the school is moving into the twenty-first century by installing its own website.

TOP LEFT *Prince William's first day at Eton. His parents and brother Harry came to see him installed in his new school.*

BOTTOM LEFT *William signs the roll-book on his first day at Eton in September 1995. Although it has never been officially confirmed he appears to be left-handed.*

RIGHT & LEFT *William in his Eton uniform of black tail coat, waist-coat, pin-striped trousers, wing collar and bow tie. The uniform originated as mourning clothes for King George III, in 1820. Eton boys have worn it ever since.*

ABOVE *William on the rugby field. He is also a keen footballer, tennis player and swimmer.*

LEFT *Prince William takes on another sport and becomes a royal 'wet bob' – Eton slang for an oarsman.*

Aged fourteen, skiing at Klosters. The solitude of the mountains around the Swiss resort appeals to Prince Charles, who spends at least a week there each year. Now his sons have come to love Klosters, too.

FOLLOWING PAGES *Prince William with school friends outside the Eton boathouse. Oarsmanship is a traditional sport at Eton. Their boating song 'Swing, Swing Together', written by a schoolmaster in the nineteenth century, is still sung by the boys.*

ABOVE *Prince William rides a jet-ski at St Tropez in July 1997*
when he and Harry, with their mother, were the guests of Mohammed
al Fayed. It was on this holiday that the Princess met Dodi Fayed.

LEFT *Both William and Harry are keen tennis*
players and regularly play at Highgrove, school
or a London sports club.

LEFT *This is typical of William's dress style — 'something baggy, soft and slouchy' and ideal for hanging out with friends near the river.*

RIGHT *Before this picture was taken William had tried to avoid the waiting cameras at the Guard's Polo Club, Windsor. But his father decided he must face up to them.*

ABOVE *Prince William, aged thirteen, wears a smart new suit to help his great-grandmother, the Queen Mother, celebrate her ninety-fifth birthday at Clarence House.*

RIGHT *Spanning the generations. Prince William escorts his great-grandmother to meet the crowds outside Clarence House.*

PREVIOUS PAGES *William relaxes with the family dogs at Balmoral.*

ABOVE *Prince Charles wearing the Balmoral tartan worn only by men of the Royal Family, with his sons in casual clothes.*

RIGHT *William on Deeside. He loves the peace and solitude of Balmoral and the shooting and deer-stalking. He is already a crack shot which pleases his grandfather, the Duke of Edinburgh.*

William with members of the Royal Family aboard the royal yacht Britannia.

William and his cousin Peter Phillips, son of the Princess Royal and her former husband Mark Phillips, share a joke aboard the royal yacht Britannia *in August 1997, at the start of the Royal Family's last voyage in her before the yacht was decommissioned. The Queen used to love the family parties aboard the yacht, and generations of royal children were taught to water-ski and scuba dive by the crew members.*

LEFT *Prince William jokes about his bouquet of yellow flowers presented to him at the Royal Naval College, Greenwich, in November 1997.*

ABOVE *A quiet reflective moment on a visit to the Naval College at Greenwich. William's increasing maturity and knowledge of the real world bodes well for the monarchy.*

ABOVE *The Prince of Wales with his sons views the carpet of flowers sent as tributes to Diana, Princess of Wales and displayed outside her home at Kensington Palace. Realizing his mother was so adored was both intensely moving and thought-provoking for her elder son.*

RIGHT *Deep in thought, Prince William leaves Westminster Abbey after his mother's funeral. He had just heard his uncle Earl Spencer vow, in his oration, to ensure that William and Harry would not be 'simply immersed by duty and tradition but can sing openly as [you] planned'.*

*The Duke of Edinburgh, Prince William, Earl Spencer, Prince Harry
and the Prince of Wales walk behind the gun carriage carrying the coffin
of Diana, Princess of Wales through London streets to Westminster Abbey.*

ABOVE AND RIGHT *The Prince of Wales and his sons, William and Harry, attend the Spiceworld première in December 1997. Both boys are fans of the Spice Girls who have appeared at shows in aid of the Prince's Trust, and William is said to have especially enjoyed the prospect of meeting Baby Spice.*

ABOVE & RIGHT *William and Harry collect gaily wrapped presents
from the crowds as they leave church at Sandringham on Christmas
morning – their first Christmas spent without their mother.*

LEFT *Seventeen-year-old Zara Phillips ready to begin a day in the mountains around Klosters with her cousin William.*

ABOVE *William skiing at Klosters in January 1998. The Prince of Wales gathered together a party of his old friends and their young as company for his sons.*

The cream of Canada's teeny-boppers all line up to give William a tumultuous welcome to their country.

At sixteen he is already a pin-up superstar. William working the crowds in Canada.

LEFT & ABOVE *Baptism of fire in Canada. William looks stunned by all the attention he receives and took a lot of teasing from his younger brother.*

LEFT *William is gradually being groomed for his future role and should be well equipped to cope with the extraordinary amount of attention he increasingly attracts. On the 1998 Canadian visit he had a few engagements with Prince Charles and Harry before escaping to the mountains for a family skiing holiday.*

ABOVE *William waves as he flies off alone by helicopter. He cannot travel by air with his father since they are both so close to the throne.*

*Just after this picture was taken Wills and Harry put their bright
red baseball caps on back to front to the approval of the audience.*

RIGHT *William wearing his newly presented
'Roots' Canadian Olympic jacket at the
Pacific Heritage Legacy on his Canadian visit
in March 1998 when teenage crowds coined
the word 'Willsmania'.*

CHRONOLOGY

21 June 1982 Prince William of Wales, eldest son and heir of the Prince of Wales and the late Diana, Princess of Wales (née Spencer) was born at 9.03 pm in the private Lindo Wing of St Mary's Hospital, Paddington, London.

4 August 1982 On the eighty-second birthday of his great-grandmother, the Queen Mother, the baby Prince was christened William Arthur Philip Louis and baptised with water from the River Jordan in the Music Room of Buckingham Palace.

March 1983 Prince William flew with his parents for a six-week visit to Australia and New Zealand.

15 September 1984 William's brother Harry was born, also in the Lindo Wing of St Mary's. He was christened Henry Charles Albert David.

September 1985 William begins school. First Mrs Mynor's nursery school not far from Kensington Palace, then in January 1987 to Wetherby, a preparatory day school in Notting Hill, London.

September 1990 William starts as a boarder at Ludgrove Preparatory School in Wokingham, Berkshire.

June 1991 William was accidentally hit on the head with a golf club by a school friend and, later, a 'routine operation' was performed at the Great Ormond Street Hospital for Sick Children in London.

March 1992 William's grandfather, Earl Spencer, dies while the Wales family is on a skiing holiday in Lech, Austria. The Prince and Princess leave William and Harry and fly back to the UK, but they are seen to be barely on speaking terms at the funeral.

December 1992 The Prince and Princess of Wales agree to separate. William and Harry, both away at school, are told the news by their mother.

September 1995   William starts his first term at Eton.

November 1995   Diana's interview on *Panorama* is broadcast. She is said to have warned William about this beforehand.

28 August 1996   A decree absolute is granted and the marriage of William's parents is over.

March 1997   The family is united again briefly for William's confirmation into the Church of England.

June 1997   Following a suggestion by William, Diana auctions a number of her dresses and raises three-and-a-half million pounds for charity and AIDS research.

July 1997   Last holiday with their mother. William and Harry go to the South of France as the guests of Mohammed al Fayed.

31 August 1997   William is awakened in the early hours in his bedroom at Balmoral, the Queen's Scottish home, to be told his mother has died in Paris in a car crash.

6 September 1997   William attends his mother's funeral at Westminster Abbey. He and his younger brother walk with their father, grandfather and uncle behind the cortège through the streets of London. Afterwards they travel to the Princess's old home at Althorp where she is laid to rest.

Easter 1998   A family skiing holiday in Canada with his father and brother saw William emerging as the next royal superstar.

21 June 1998   William's sixteenth birthday.

First BENFORD BOOKS edition 1998
Published by Benford Books
234 Nassau St.
Princeton, New Jersey 08542

First published in Great Britain in 1998 by Weidenfeld & Nicolson

ISBN 1-56649-050-2
M 10 9 8 7 6 5 4 3 2 1

Library of Congress information available from the Publisher

Printed and Bound in Great Britain by
Butler & Tanner Ltd, Frome and London
Set in Monotype Bembo

Weidenfeld & Nicolson
The Orion Publishing Group Ltd
5 Upper Saint Martin's Lane
London WC2H 9EA

Photograph Acknowledgements:
All Action: 19; All Action/Mark Cuthbert: 83; All Action/Terry Hillfry: 41(b); All
Action/Dennis James: 12; All Action/Rod King: 57; All Action/Duncan Raban:
36; Alpha/Dave Chancellor: 14, 58–9, 60, 61, 69; Alpha/Steve Daniels: 6, 27,
86(t&b), 87, 89, 90; Big Pictures: 23, 80, 82, 88, 89; Camera Press: 9, 40(t), 42,
66–67; CP/Peter Abbey/LNS: 31(t&b); CP/G. Barlow: 30(t); CP/J. Bennett: 28;
CP/Richard Gillard: 25, 45, 48; CP/Glenn Harvey: 30(b), 35; CP/N. Hinkes:
40(b); CP/SOA: 13; CP/Stewart Mark: 22, 47, 50, 52 (t), 64; CP/B Morton: 41(t);
CP/R. Open: 39; CP/Snowdon: 29, 32–33, 34; CP/John Swannell: 10, 43;
Express Newspapers: 74; Mirror Syndication: 76(b), 77, 84; Nunn Syndication
Ltd/Robin Nunn: 2, 79, 92, 93; Nunn Syndicatin Ltd/ Kelvin Bruce: 16, 62, 75,
78; PA News/Rebecca Naden: 76(t); PA News/John Stillwell: 70–71, 72–73; Pap-
pix UK: 56(t); Photographer's International/Jayne Fincher: 1, 37, 38, 52(b), 54,
63, 65, 68, 85; Rex Features: 46; Rex Features/Jim Bennett: 56(b); Rex Fea-
tures/David Hartley: 51; Rex Features/Tim Rooke: 4, 81; Universal Pictorial
Press & Agency Ltd: 20, 44, 55